PROJECTS IN
Ethnographic
RESEARCH

Michael V. Angrosino
University of South Florida

WAVELAND

PRESS, INC.

Long Grove, Illinois

For information about this book, contact:
Waveland Press, Inc.
4180 IL Route 83, Suite 101
Long Grove, IL 60047-9580
(847) 634-0081
info@waveland.com
www.waveland.com

Contents

Preface   v

1   Ethnographic Methods and Social Research   1
What Is Ethnography?   4
Using This Book   9
Key Terms   10

2   Basic Principles of Ethnographic Research   11
Ethics   19
Key Terms   21   ◆   To Do!   21   ◆   Notes   22

**3   Site Selection and
Other Practical Considerations   23**
Units of Analysis   23
Selection Criteria   25
Some Practical Considerations   26
First Contact   27
Some Personal Considerations   28
Key Terms   29   ◆   To Do!   30   ◆   Note   31

4 Ethnographic Observation **33**
Getting Started   33
Types of Observation   37
Key Terms 39 ◆ *To Do! 40* ◆ *Notes 41*

5 Ethnographic Interviewing **43**
Types of Ethnographic Interviews   44
Key Terms 51 ◆ *To Do! 52* ◆ *Notes 53*

**6 Ethnography and the
Analysis of Archived Materials** **55**
Key Terms 59 ◆ *To Do! 59* ◆ *Notes 60*

7 Presenting Your Findings **61**
To Do! 64

Additional Reading   65

Index   69

Preface

TO INSTRUCTORS

This manual is designed to give even beginning students a taste of what it is like to *do* ethnographic research. It is meant to supplement class lectures on the substantive data of the social sciences. It is also assumed that one or more published ethnographies will be assigned for student reading, and that there will be exams or other assignments depending on your pedagogical preferences. Under those circumstances, it is highly unlikely that any of you will want to assign all the "To Do" projects suggested in the book—although selected individual students pursuing honors might complete all the exercises as a basis for producing a piece of research leading to a senior thesis. You are therefore urged to review all the exercises carefully and select only those that most closely fit your course plan. Many of the exercises have suggested word or page lengths, but these parameters can be expanded or limited at your own discretion.

TO STUDENTS

This manual was written by someone who has been conducting ethnographic research of one sort or another for more than three decades. I continue to be excited by the ways in which these methods get us involved with real people in real-life situations, and thus help us learn something about their lives (and, by implication, about our own circumstances as well).

Doing ethnography comes naturally, in a sense, because most of its specific methods are based on ways we act in everyday life (e.g., observing our surroundings, engaging in conversation, looking up background information on topics that particularly interest us). But as you will see, doing ethnography is an act of social science research requiring some attention to detail that we can afford to gloss over in everyday life. Treat this manual, then, as an invitation to systematize your way of interacting with people in social settings in order to gain some insight into how social scientists go about finding out all that fascinating stuff you read about in your textbooks.

In working through this manual, be sure to rely on your instructor for guidance and support. He or she will be assigning particular exercises for you to complete, either individually or in groups, although I hope you will take at least a brief look at the unassigned exercises in order to get a feeling for the range of skills you might want someday to develop. Your instructor will also assist you in selecting research settings and topics that are not only interesting to you, but "do-able" given local circumstances.

Above all, have fun as you look at the data of social science with a fresh perspective that comes with new insight into how ethnographers proceed to learn about the material in your textbooks and class lectures.

ACKNOWLEDGMENTS

This book owes its existence to the encouragement and good advice provided by Thomas Curtin, the anthropology editor of Waveland Press. I am very grateful for the guidance and support he has provided me over the course of several projects undertaken over the years for Waveland.

The material in this book reflects nearly three decades of teaching ethnographic methods at all levels of the anthropology curriculum, as well as in courses on ethnographic methods offered for students in education, public health, and the interdisciplinary honors program. The content has been shaped and refined by the experiences of literally hundreds of students over the years, but I would like to extend special thanks to Roseanne Brophy and Emmett Daigner for helping me distill those experiences into the exercises presented herein.

William Hare, Rita Sakitt, and Steve Froemming all read early drafts of the manuscript and provided excellent, constructive criticism. I am indebted to them for helping make this book stronger, although I accept all responsibility for any perceived shortcomings in the final product. I also acknowledge the clerical and editorial assistance of Petra LeClair and Kate Brelsford.

Ethnographic Methods and Social Research

I write this book as one who has been studying and teaching anthropology for more than three decades and who has a deep, abiding, and unabashed love for the discipline. But even I must admit that anthropology can sometimes be difficult to embrace. Certainly there's the initial rush of excitement over learning about how people in faraway places and in ancient times lived their lives and thought about the world around them. There is also the challenge of finding out something of how we as a species came to be and where we fit into the larger pattern of life on the planet. There is even the thrill of the prospect of being able to use our knowledge of human behavior to contribute to the solution of important problems in our own place and time. But then we open a textbook in introductory anthropology only to be confronted with seemingly endless lists of fossil hominids, bewildering kinship diagrams, hundreds of pages of unfamiliar names, and an apparently mind-numbing array of detailed facts and figures concerning every conceivable aspect of the human condition. Anthropology is, after all, about all things human, and that's a tall order. As humans, we're naturally curious to learn as much about ourselves as we can—but can we really make it all the way through a formal study of anthropology?

For many of us, studying anthropology isn't as hard as, say, nuclear physics, since it at least deals with things that are recognizable to anyone even minimally aware of the wide world of people and their customs. But that perception may contribute to the frustration. At its heart anthropology deals with the fundamental stuff of everyday life (making a living, figuring out relationships, finding ways to cooperate, wondering about truth and beauty), and so it is easy to feel exasperated when all that potentially interesting insight gets buried under technical jargon and far more descriptive and analytical detail than anyone can ever hope to master.

I can say quite honestly that I have long since stopped thinking that I could ever learn everything about all things anthropological. Even after all these years I still consider myself a student. But as a student who is also a professor, I take it as an important part of my duty to help beginners sort through the complexities and think about what really matters. Mind you, I am not saying that we can or should avoid the complexities. But we can learn to ask some of the questions that will make them seem less of a barrier and more of a pathway to understanding.

One thing I have learned as a professor is that students of any age at whatever level tend to learn facts, figures, and concepts best when they can actually experience the process that led to the discovery of those facts, figures, and concepts. One of the problems in most introductory texts is that they are crammed with statements that are presented as facts to be remembered. There's nothing wrong with remembering facts, but I always encourage my students to interrogate such material: whenever presented by something that seems to be unadorned "fact," whether by the author of the textbook or by me in a lecture, they should ask, "How do they know that? How did they find that out? What would it be like to live in the circumstances in which anthropologists find themselves in order to answer such questions?" In other words, I want students to ask how an anthropologist actually does his or her job so that the raw material of everyday existence comes to be translated into the "facts" presented in a textbook.

It is one thing to ask you hypothetically what it would be like to do anthropology or what might be involved in coming to know something presented as a fact to be memorized. It is all the more persuasive if you can experience a bit of what it means to do research for yourselves. Many of you who are using this manual are not prepared to conduct extensive research projects on your own—certainly not while you are taking courses or are otherwise involved in the activities of normal life. But small-scale guided exercises can give you a hint of what fully realized research is like.

It is just such exercises that form the core of this book, and they are presented as ways in which you can begin to answer the question "How do they *know* that?" The exercises are to be conducted under your instructor's supervision—he or she will know best what local circumstances lend themselves to the suggested activities. Most activities can be accomplished either by individual students or as group efforts, depending on the size of the class or other considerations in the instructor's pedagogical plan. In any case, an important part of the learning process will be for you to come together as a class (or in small groups within large classes) to share what you have learned. It is a fine thing to learn something new; it is perhaps even better to be able to convey what you've learned (both the substance of the thing and the excitement you may have felt while figuring it out) to others. Both are part of the process of critical thinking. By "critical" I do not mean being negatively judgmental; *critical thinking* is the act of probing beneath the surface of things that appear to be settled and taken for granted. At the end of a process of critical reflection you may well end up reaffirming things you already thought you knew, but at least you will be on firmer ground in asserting your position because you know what is involved in getting to that position.

What Is Ethnography?

All anthropologists are interested in *cultures*, integrated systems of ideas, behaviors, and material products that typify the way of life of a group of people. When we focus on the ways of living people, we are studying *cultural anthropology*. In one way or another, to one degree or another, cultural anthropologists make use of the *ethnographic method* in the study of living people. It is important, however, to keep in mind that the ethnographic method is no longer the exclusive preserve of cultural anthropologists. Researchers in other social sciences (e.g., sociology, social psychology, communication, geography), in education, business, public health, and nursing have become enthusiastic boosters of ethnography to the extent that the issues they deal with can be defined as matters of "culture" in one way or another.

Ethnography literally means the description ("-graphy") of a people ("ethnos"). So in one sense an ethnography is a narrative account of a people and its way of life. By tradition, most ethnographies have been written in the form of books or articles in standard scientific prose. However, some ethnographic reports have taken the form of films/videos, collections of photos, museum displays, or performance pieces involving music, dance, or poetry. But the word "ethnography" also refers to a process—the means by which a researcher collects and interprets information. We will focus on this sense of the word for most of this book, although we will return to the matter of ethnography as a descriptive account in chapter 7.

Ethnographers use their methods in "the field," meaning the settings in which people conduct their everyday lives. "The field" is therefore different from a laboratory or clinical setting in which other kinds of social scientists conduct research. In the latter, researchers are in control of most of the elements in the research situation—they choose the people to be studied, place them in conditions that reflect their hypotheses, and do not bother to answer questions about those aspects of the people's lives that are seen as extraneous to the research question at hand. By contrast, the "field" is a kind of "natural laboratory." Researchers will still have their own agendas, but carrying out the research depends on a number of factors they cannot control. Within this realm, *field research* is conducted. As people go about their business, they may or may not exhibit the behaviors or engage in the kinds of activities that the researcher finds most germane to the research—or they may do so at times or in ways that are not especially convenient for the researcher. People may be less willing than the researcher might like to allow access to their private lives. And even in the best of situations—if the people are warmly welcoming and try to arrange things to suit their understanding of the researcher's needs—the entire enterprise is surrounded by all the "extraneous" things the lab-based researcher works so hard to set aside. Real life, after all, can be quite messy and is never really organized in the manner of a rigorous experimental design.

Ethnographic methods have therefore developed in ways that result from their application in this messy "natural laboratory." The lab-based experimental researcher is supposed to interact as little as possible with the people under study. But in the field, the researcher is immersed in the lives of real people, and so the questions asked and the situations observed must necessarily be the product of the encounter of particular people at a particular time in a particular set of circumstances. When it comes to experimental research and ethnographic research, one is inherently neither better nor worse than the other. They serve different purposes and answer different kinds of questions. Ethnographers are usually *participants* in as well as *observers* of the people they study. It is possible to use ethnographic methods in situations that differ from those in the "natural laboratory" described in this section, but for the most part they are applied by researchers who do consider themselves "participant-observers" in the field. See chapter 4 for more information about participant observation.

Experimental researchers, by controlling the factors involved in the research setting, can work with a limited set of variables that can be very precisely defined and for which quantified measures can be devised. (These procedures are referred to as the *operationalization* of variables.) Ethnographers can certainly generate numerical data, but a relatively large chunk of the information they collect takes the form of open-ended, descriptive, narrative responses that sometimes defy reasonable efforts at quantification. *Interpretive research* yields ethnographic data that lend themselves to *interpretation* rather than to statistically validated statements of cause or association. Learning about the culture of a people can sometimes have more in common with the way in which a literary scholar studies a novel than the way in which an experimental researcher works with precise statistical correlations. Ethnographers, therefore, are primarily interested in *qualitative research* questions that probe for interpretations rather than for definitive associations, such as, "What does it *mean* (e.g., to espouse "family values") in this community?" or "What is it *like* (e.g., to be a single parent) in this community?" To be sure, literary scholars look for patterns and associations, as do ethnographers. The main difference is that they do not always use the sort of quantified data that lend themselves to the generation of statistical correlations to establish those patterns and associations.

For these reasons, ethnographers themselves are the primary instruments of research. In the objective world of experimental design, there is a basic assumption that a methodology devised to test a certain hypothesis could be applied by any competent researcher: the research would always yield the same results no matter who conducted the experiment. But in the field, ethnographers must always be aware of who they are as people beyond their technical expertise as researchers. There are some characteristics that field researchers can and do learn to change to suit the needs and expectations of the people they aim to study; they can, for example, modify the kind of clothes or jewelry they wear, and they can be conscious of aspects of personal grooming that fit the norms of the community in which they are functioning as participant-observers. They can take steps to make sure that their tone of voice, body language, and repertoire of gestures are in keeping with what the people being studied would consider proper. But on the other hand, there are some characteristics that we can't do much about: our gender, relative age, perceived racial or ethnic category, for example. The best we can do with these factors is to gauge how they might be interpreted by the people being studied and perhaps even to step aside if it appears that they will be a real barrier to gaining rapport. An African American, for example, might well be interested in learning why certain whites remain bitterly racist in their thinking, but it is highly unlikely that he or she would be able to arrange a successful participant observation study in a community of bigots. (Rapport will be discussed in more detail in chapter 2.)

Ethnographers must also be aware of their own limits as instruments of research. There is a romantic notion that a good ethnographer must be willing to deal bravely with any and all hardships. But being a good sport certainly has its limits. If you are a person with serious sensitivity to cold you would be ill-advised to plan to do fieldwork in the Canadian Arctic. If for whatever reason you are a committed vegan, you should probably not think of doing research among people whose religious life is centered around feasts that involve animal sacrifice. If you have strong personal moral objections to corporal punishment, multiple marriages, homosexuality, premarital sex, etc., then you would probably be highly uncomfortable doing field research where such things are routinely practiced. It is, of course, a good thing to test your own limits and get out of your familiar "comfort zone," but it may not be feasible for you to do so within the scope of the time-limited exercises in this book. When deciding what to do to complete the suggested exercises in this book, do *not* feel that you *must* do something that tests the outer limits of your tolerance.

It's no wonder that the process of doing ethnographic fieldwork is both tantalizingly glamorous and forbiddingly esoteric to the beginning student. Going out into the community—even one that's just in another part of town, let alone halfway around the world—can seem more truly exciting than going down to a laboratory in the basement to watch people through one-way glass, or sitting by the mailbox waiting to get responses to a questionnaire. But at the same time, going out into the community can be a scary thing: Suppose they don't like me? Suppose nobody talks to me? Suppose nothing interesting happens during the time I'm there? And even if things look promising, then what? What, when it comes right down to it, does an ethnographer *do* in the field?

For a very long time, cultural anthropologists and other practitioners of the ethnographic method were inclined to be rather mysterious when it came to doing fieldwork. There was a kind of clubby secret-adventure mystique to it all. Students were sent off with minimal formal preparation to do field-work—if they came back with data for a dissertation, then all well and good; if they didn't come back, well, they just didn't have the right stuff. It should have been obvious that doing field research must always have amounted to more than packing your bags, landing in the middle of nowhere, and hoping for the best. But unlike "objective" experimental researchers, who have long been very careful to make their methodology "transparent," ethnographers have preferred to pretend that things just sort of happen.

Well, in fact they don't just happen, as the growing prominence of textbooks, manuals, and guides to ethnographic research amply demonstrates. Ethnographic field research does indeed have a heavy dose of serendipity to it, but it is also based on sound principles of how to collect and analyze information. Fieldwork is definitely more than haphazard wishing for things to turn out well. There must be a set of skills that people from different disciplines can learn so that they can produce those ethnographies that give us our lived-in glimpses of the lives of people who are in some measure different from ourselves. If you compare ethnographies written before the 1970s to those written after, you will also notice a real change: nowadays, researchers are much more forthcoming about their own experiences in the field. The enduring popularity of such ethnographies as Napoleon Chagnon's Yanomamo series or Richard Lee's accounts of the Dobe !Kung (Dobe Ju/wasi) is due in no small measure to the vivid personalities of those scholars—they are clearly part of the story, not simply emotionally neutral, god-like observers from afar. For that reason, those books (and any number of others in that genre) are often assigned to supplement introductory texts; they really do help the student see some of what it takes to collect and make sense out of the impressions that ultimately wind up as "facts" in the textbook.

But such books still tell only part of the story. The basic premise of this book is that even beginning students can only truly learn how to do ethnography by doing it themselves. Memorizing the facts and figures from textbooks and living the field experience vicariously through the reports of selected ethnographic authors are both fine ways to get started. But the missing piece of the puzzle is allowing newcomers to experience what it's like out in the field, so that they come to know firsthand "how do they know that?"

Using This Book

This book is designed to function as a module within a larger series of topics in basic cultural anthropology. In one sense, it is an expansion of the traditional textbook chapter on field research. But in this case, the material is not presented simply as additional externalized facts and figures to memorize, but as guided steps in the firsthand experience of what it is like to be in the field and to participate directly in the generation of interesting knowledge about people and their cultures. As such any newcomer to the world of ethnographic research—whether in anthropology or any of the other disciplines in which such research has come to the fore—can participate in the generation of knowledge by completing the suggested exercises in this book.

In chapter 2, we will overview some of the basic principles of ethnographic research and look at a few examples of ethnographies conducted close to "home" (to counteract the stereotype that ethnography is only conducted in "exotic" locales). This chapter will also introduce some of the main data collection techniques that are associated with participant observation and the ethnographic method in general. Ethical considerations in conducting ethnographic research will also be considered.

Chapter 3 will include some pointers for selecting suitable locations for local ethnographic field research. Final decisions about this matter (as they pertain to the exercises from this book that are assigned during a semester) must, however, necessarily be left to the discretion of the course instructor. But the heart of the book will be in a set of projects that beginning students can undertake (under their instructors' careful guidance, of course) for themselves. For purposes of this presentation, we will define the broad category of ethnography in terms of three basic operations that a good field researcher must master. In one way or another, all of the many ethnographic data collection techniques are variants of:

▲ observation

▲ interviewing

▲ analyzing archives

Therefore, in chapter 4 students will be given projects designed to hone their skills in observation; in chapter 5 the projects will be based on interviewing; and in chapter 6 they will deal with archival research. In each chapter, exercises will be suggested that can be carried out either by an individual student or by a team, depending on the preference of the instructor. Depending on other course assignments, the instructor may select only some of the exercises, although the ideal would be to have the class follow them all in sequence.

The exercises (whether they are individual projects or group efforts) should be carried out in the same community if at all possible. At the end of the semester, the instructor may choose to build in some way for each student (or each team) to share the fruits of research with the rest of the class—and, if feasible, with members of the study community. Chapter 7 offers some creative and beneficial options for doing so.

KEY TERMS

Be sure you can define and explain the importance of the following terms:

◆ critical thinking
◆ cultural anthropology
◆ cultures
◆ ethnographic method

◆ ethnography
◆ field research
◆ interpretive research
◆ qualitative research

Basic Principles of Ethnographic Research

The previous chapter introduced some of the ways in which ethnographic research differs from other kinds of social research. In this chapter we will take a closer look at the concepts, approaches, and assumptions that characterize the use of ethnographic methods.

First, ethnographic research presupposes a "natural laboratory" (the field) rather than a laboratory or clinic as the locus of study. Ethnographers are interested in studying people in the settings in which they actually live, work, and play rather than settings that are specifically designed to meet the demands of a researcher's hypotheses. For example, much of my own research over the past two decades has focused on adults with mental retardation and/or chronic mental illness. Since the 1980s such people have been treated mainly in local communities rather than in large institutions. Most researchers who are interested in this population take a clinical perspective and they tend to gauge the success or failure of a client's "deinstitutionalization" by means of controlled observations at treatment facilities or highly focused interviews by medical or social work professionals. As an anthropologist, however, I have been more interested in what it is like for a person diagnosed with a mental "disability" who must make his or her way in the community beyond the protective walls of the state hospitals of yesteryear; I also wanted to know what the concept of "disability" itself meant—not to the professionals who write the clinical manuals, but to the people who must live with the label on a day-to-day basis. As a result, I have conducted ethnographic research with deinstitutionalized adults in several communities (both urban and semi-rural) around the United States. I have been a participant-observer in sheltered workshops, training facilities, group homes, and at supervised job sites. I have attended social events of various kinds in the company of my study populations. My research does not yield answers to important clinical questions (such as which medications are most successful in alleviating psychiatric symptoms), but I do have answers to equally important social and cultural questions. I learned, for example, that clients were particularly concerned with learning about managing their sexuality, because they believed that this factor, even more than academic and job skills, made them able to function with reasonable success as adults in the "real world."[1]

Second, ethnography usually requires personal contact between the researcher and the members of the study community. In other words, the researcher is not simply "the researcher" who relates to his or her "subjects" only in that one dimension. The ethnographer becomes, as much as is feasible, a part of the everyday life of the people being studied. Ideally, the ethnographer becomes such a familiar presence that his or her research agenda is no longer even consciously on the minds of community members. Ethnographers must therefore seek to establish real *rapport* with the people they study—not just the ordinary trust they might inspire as competent researchers, but a real friendship that is based on their personal as well as their professional qualities. The process of establishing rapport continues throughout the life of a research project—it is not something that happens in one fell swoop.

Establishing rapport is vital to ethnographic research precisely because the method is based on personal contact rather than the objective distancing typical of experimental research. Essential to the rapport-building process is the notion of *mutuality.* The researcher is, after all, asking a lot of the people he or she is studying—they are being coaxed to share private information as well as a considerable amount of time. It is therefore only fair that the researcher be willing to reciprocate in some way. In some cases, doing so might take the form of cash remuneration. This solution is rarely considered desirable, however, as it not only might be beyond the financial resources of a researcher, but it might put the relationship on a depersonalized level that violates the essence of rapport. For those reasons, mutuality is more often expressed in terms of reciprocal social arrangements—for example, the researcher might drive people to appointments, babysit their children, treat them to meals. The researcher should also be prepared to share some of the same kinds of private information that he or she is asking of community members; the ethnographer, for example, should be prepared to show pictures of family or friends, or talk about events or relationships important in his or her life.

One of my graduate students was interested in the ways in which African American women with diabetes managed their treatment (i.e., to what extent they followed their doctors' recommendations about modifying diet and exercise, taking medications, and monitoring glucose levels). She decided to do this research because a close relative had recently passed away due to complications from diabetes and she wanted to learn as much as she could to help people of her own community make the most of available health care. At the outset, however, she thought it would be best to rely on her professional status (she has an extensive background in public health as well as in anthropology). Although the women she met at various community clinics were cordial to her, they were not altogether forthcoming with their information. It was not until she began sharing her feelings about the death of her loved one that the women in the community recognized an emotional link with her. Once she opened up to them, they opened up to her and her ability to collect richly contextualized (as opposed to merely clinical) data was greatly enhanced.

This student developed a role for herself in the community with her own initiative. It is also possible, however, to work toward rapport in a more structured way. For example, the anthropologist Elizabeth Grobsmith has long specialized in studying the concerns of Native Americans who are incarcerated. Her involvement began back in the 1970s when a U.S. District Court in Nebraska allowed Native Americans to practice their religion (and other aspects of their traditional culture) while in jail. The decree also allowed the prisoners access to culture-specific education and, with the assistance of the state's Indian Commission, provided academic programs in American Indian studies. Grobsmith began as a teacher in one such program, and over the course of time her expert professional contributions to a course of action endorsed by the Indian prisoners resulted in a fund of trust and goodwill. This kind of report might not otherwise have been forthcoming to a non-Native American seeking to do research with such a population.[2]

Third, ethnographic research seeks the perspectives and meanings held by members of the study community. To be sure, all research begins with a researcher whose studies have led him or her to believe that a certain issue merits investigation. But expert outsider perspectives, no matter how well informed by a global, comparative view, should not stand as the whole story. People involved in a social situation will inevitably have their own take on what is going on in their lives, and this inside view, which ethnographic methods are particularly well-suited to elicit, should be an important part of a description of a culture.

The anthropologist Philippe Bourgois, for example, studied crack dealers in New York City. While most observers would see this phenomenon as a social problem, Bourgois wanted to learn how the dealers saw themselves—did they think of themselves as criminals or social deviants? He found out that the dealers preferred to see themselves as entrepreneurs; in an inner-city community lacking viable economic options for young men, selling drugs was a way to earn money and hence to acquire desirable goods as well as prestige. Bourgois's vivid description of this insider perspective certainly does not alter the fact that the outside world continues to evaluate drug dealers in harshly negative terms. But it does give us some unaccustomed insight into the ways in which people can find positive benefits in an activity that might otherwise be seen as having no redeeming value at all. It suggests that one way to conduct a "war on drugs" is not to inveigh against the immorality of the practice but to provide economic options that might make dealing less attractive as a career path for bright, ambitious young people.[3]

Fourth, ethnographic research is designed to generate data so as to build general theories. In the language of the philosophy of science, ethnographic research is an *inductive inquiry* that operates out of a framework sometimes referred to as *grounded theory*. It is certainly possible to conduct scientific research the other way around: *deductive inquiry* is a process in which one starts with an established theory from which testable hypotheses can be derived. But when working in the relatively open-ended "field" where there are no controlled variables, it is usually more practical to begin with general research questions (rather than formal hypotheses) that can be explored through a variety of data collection techniques. This process continues until new information builds into a clear pattern that supports a general explanation of an event or behavior. (A *theory* in social science is, quite simply, a way to explain a perceived pattern in events and behaviors.) Inductive inquiry in ethnography is therefore associated with a technique known as *triangulation*: using multiple means to collect data from a variety of sources (e.g., the observations, interviews, and archival materials that you are learning about in this manual) so that the researcher can close in on the ultimate general explanatory model from the widest possible set of perspectives.

For example, sociologist Gary Dworkin was interested in the phenomenon of teacher burnout, but he was unimpressed with the prevailing theories he had read about, most of them formulated by psychologists who focused on the dynamics of individual stress. Dworkin conducted extensive ethnographic fieldwork in public schools in various parts of the United States, interviewing many teachers, students, and administrators and observing many different schools in different types of social settings. He learned that the stress that leads to burnout has less to do with insufficiencies within the individual teachers and more to do with structural or institutional problems inherent in the way public schools are run in modern society. It is the feeling that "the rules have all changed and I cannot do anything about it" that generates the stress leading to burnout.[4]

Fifth, ethnographic research always seeks to understand the *context* of behavior, and not simply the content of that behavior. A social and/or cultural context is the sum total of all the factors (people, groups, institutions, history, economics, politics, the physical environment) that influence the behavior and beliefs of people. Anthropologists traditionally refer to this principle as a ***holistic perspective***. A medical doctor, for example, might see a patient's diabetes as a result of an organic breakdown in the insulin-producing cells and would treat only those physical symptoms. A social researcher would look for predisposing factors that constitute the context of the patient's condition and that exacerbate this physical disease (e.g., limited dietary choices available in a poor community).

In a different kind of project, the anthropologist Constance deRoche was interested in the ways in which a small, rural fishing community in Nova Scotia, Canada, had adapted to the new economic opportunities provided by the opening of an industrial park just a few miles away. It would be a relatively simple matter to document the purely economic changes (reflected in salary patterns, household expenditures, and so forth), but deRoche realized that in a close-knit, traditional community such as this village it would be necessary to understand the more extensive context in which these economic changes had come about. For one thing, it turned out that the villagers had a long-standing pattern of emigrating elsewhere for wage employment (either temporarily or permanently); but no matter how often or how far they went away from home, they maintained very strong ties to the home town. Indeed, it was impossible to understand the patterns of economic opportunity just by looking at local employment options—it was necessary to understand something about the kinship patterns, which in turn reflected religious beliefs and ideas about gender. In short, people were not motivated purely by economic opportunism; a number of people in the study community had, in fact, chosen to stay put for reasons of tradition that, in their own minds, outweighed the economic advantages of going away.[5]

Sixth, ethnography is predicated on an understanding of culture. In the previous chapter we defined a culture as a kind of system—an integrated set of beliefs, behaviors, and material products that is shared by a particular people. Thus, it is not individual behavior, except insofar as an individual can be seen as a representative of a more extensive pattern. An ethnographic researcher is therefore not interested in merely recording specific acts or expressions, he or she wants to see how those factors fit together in a systematic way so as to constitute a culture. We cannot assume that a culture is a ready-made phenomenon that is easy to identify. For example, a certain neighborhood in a city might be inhabited primarily by people defined by the census as "Hispanic." Although such people might share a number of traits, the defining characteristic of this category is that they all speak Spanish. But important as language is to cultural identity, it is never the sum total of culture. "Hispanics" in the United States derive from many different parts of the world (Mexico, Puerto Rico, various countries in the Caribbean, Central and South America, to name just a few); local traditions might well override any solidarity implied by the shared language. Moreover, in the United States "Hispanics" are divided by social class, occupation, educational attainment, religious affiliation, and so on. We should not assume that there is a unitary "Hispanic" culture just because that category is available as a single check-off box on so many government forms. The job of the ethnographer is to find out the elements that matter to people in specified communities and to see how they construct a sense of cultural identity that suits their particular needs.

Of particular importance to the ethnographic study of culture is the principle of *cultural relativism*, which means that every culture is assumed to be meaningful and useful to those who follow its ways. The ethnographer cannot possibly study culture without beginning with the assumption that whatever is observed or elicited through interviews or the study of artifacts is neither good nor bad—it just is. The principal task of the ethnographer is to *describe* and *explain*, not to judge. Being a cultural relativist does not mean that the ethnographer is not entitled to his or her opinions of what is right or wrong, just that in the course of research such opinions are set aside and the culture is allowed to speak for itself on its own terms. (In the previous chapter we pointed out that if some cultural practices are completely unacceptable to the researcher, the thing to do is diplomatically bow out—not to lecture the people about their supposed misdeeds and call them to reform.)

Since the United States is preeminently a land of immigrants, it is important to understand the cultural matrix in which people move from place to place—a process very much speeded up and facilitated by modern transportation and communication networks. Some ethnographers, such as Kathleen Murphy for example, have studied the phenomenon of the "border identity"—people from Mexico who cross into the United States to work, shop, or socialize with friends, but who return to Mexico to buy land or access social services. They are neither "Mexican" nor "American" in the stereotyped sense of those labels—they have created a culture and an identity that reflects the transitional nature of their circumstances.[6] In another case, Dianna Shandy has studied refugees from the civil war in Sudan who have been relocated by international agencies to Minnesota. They seemed to her at first to be an "incongruous" people—black herdsmen from Africa plunked down in a largely white (and cold) urban setting. But she soon learned that the refugees' desire to "make a better life" (the eternal refrain of the immigrant) encouraged them to make the best adaptation they could to these strange new surroundings. They had lost almost all the important elements of their traditional culture (raising cattle in a tropical ecology not being a replicable strategy in the heart of Minneapolis), and yet they kept a sense of themselves as a distinct people by means of a very modern piece of technology—the Internet. Shandy learned that refugees from Sudan had been resettled in as many as thirty different states in the United States, but they had created a viable strategy for keeping in touch with one another. They were also able to keep in touch with relatives back in Africa; marriages, Shandy found, were often arranged via long-distance phone calls.[7]

Ethics

Because ethnography is a process of research mediated by personal encounters, ethnographic researchers must be concerned with the ethical dimensions of their studies. Indeed, ethics is a topic treated with major emphasis in most modern considerations of the research enterprise. Like all academic disciplines, anthropology has developed a code of conduct that guides members in the conduct of research. Although the code of anthropological ethics shares many features with those of other disciplines, it has a character of its own. Because we are nonjudgmental about the people and cultures we study, we believe that our first responsibility as researchers is to respect the people we study. We need to protect their dignity, their privacy, and their interests as much as we can. To be sure, we also owe something to those who fund our research (and who expect a certain product at a certain time as an outcome), to the scholarly community in general (which expects research to contribute somehow to the fund of knowledge and understanding), and to the general public (which has a right to the information we collect). But the ethically informed anthropologist is expected to put the interests of the people studied at the top of the priority list.

Because of abuses of research (mostly in the biomedical field, but tainting other kinds of research as well), the federal government in the 1970s mandated the establishment of *Institutional Review Boards* (IRBs) at every university, hospital, museum, or other facility at which research is conducted using federal funds. The IRBs are composed of panels of experienced researchers who review every research proposal submitted by faculty, staff, and students that involves other people, and their mandate is to make sure that all research conforms to certain ethical standards. They have two overriding ethical concerns that reinforce anthropology's philosophical predisposition to respect the people under study. Those principles are informed consent and confidentiality. *Informed consent* is the process by which "human subjects" are given information sufficient for them to make a decision as to whether they freely choose to participate in a study. Agreement is indicated by the signing of a release form. *Confidentiality* is the principle of striving to protect the privacy of individual participants. Academic researchers do not enjoy the status shared by clergy, physicians, or attorneys in that their communication with the people they study is not automatically "privileged." However, we can do our best to maintain confidentiality (e.g., by making sure that no one has access to notes taken in the field, or by changing the names of participants when writing up reports), and our plans for doing so should be part of the informed consent forms that participants are asked to sign.

Ethnographers are sometimes uncomfortable with the formalities of the IRB review process. Unlike experimental researchers, ethnographers cannot always anticipate everything that is likely to happen during the course of a research project. A great deal of fieldwork happens serendipitously, as leads ethnographers may not even have suspected as important turn out to be worth pursuing. It is impossible, they say, to describe every possible contingency in an informed consent form. Some ethnographers go so far as to say that social research, unlike biomedical research, can never be truly harmful, although this is an extreme position rejected by the majority who recognize that even the best-intended research can sometimes have unintended negative consequences.

By way of a compromise, a number of universities have adopted a two-tier IRB system in which there are separate committees for biomedical and social/behavioral science research. Within this system it is possible for an ethnographic researcher to request an "expedited" review for nonclinical projects (unless they deal with certain federally designated "vulnerable" populations, namely children, the elderly, people with mental disorders, or those in prison). In any case, it is important for even the beginning researcher to be aware of the ethical dimension of research and to get into the habit of providing truly informed consent (including a feasible plan for confidentiality) for those they wish to study.

KEY TERMS

Be sure you can define and explain the importance of the following terms:

- ◆ confidentiality
- ◆ cultural relativism
- ◆ deductive inquiry
- ◆ grounded theory
- ◆ holistic perspective
- ◆ inductive inquiry

- ◆ informed consent
- ◆ Institutional Review Boards
- ◆ mutuality
- ◆ rapport
- ◆ theory
- ◆ triangulation

To do!

If you are enrolled at a research-oriented college or university, complete the project as follows:

Although class projects are normally exempt from IRB review, it is a good idea for you to begin to learn the process in anticipation of more extensive research to come. To that end, you can work either as individuals or in groups to find out what your own university's IRB process is like. With your instructor's assistance, obtain copies of at least two proposals for ethnographic research that have passed review at your university. Then conduct a class discussion of the ethical issues involved in those proposals as well as the ways in which the researchers satisfied the IRB that proper informed consent and confidentiality standards were maintained.

If you are enrolled at an educational institution without a large research component:
Select another college or university and, through its Web site, review its IRB process. Then select two or three research articles from a current issue of any social science journal and use those articles as the basis of a discussion of the ethical issues involved in the research process. If you were a member of the IRB reviewing these research efforts at the school whose procedures you studied, what would you especially make sure the researchers dealt with?

NOTES

[1] Angrosino, Michael V. 1992. "Metaphors of Stigma: How Deinstitutionalized Mentally Retarded Adults See Themselves," *Journal of Contemporary Ethnography* 21:171–99.

[2] Grobsmith, Elizabeth S. 1992. "Applying Anthropology to American Indian Correctional Concerns," *Practicing Anthropology* 14(3):5–8.

[3] Bourgois, Philippe. 1995. "Workaday World, Crack Economy," *The Nation* 261(19):706–11.

[4] Dworkin, A. Gary. 1987. *Teacher Burnout in the Public Schools: Structural Causes and Consequences for Children.* Albany: State University of New York Press.

[5] deRoche, Constance. 1985. *The Village, the Vertex: Adaptation to Regionalism and Development in a Complex Society.* Halifax, Nova Scotia: St. Mary's University Department of Anthropology (Occasional Papers in Anthropology no. 12).

[6] Murphy, Kathleen M. 2001. "Heading South: Why Mexicans and Mexican-Americans in Brownsville, Texas, Cross the Border into Mexico," *Latino Workers in the Contemporary South*, ed. Arthur D. Murphy, Colleen Blanchard, and Jennifer A. Hill (pp. 114–25). Athens: University of Georgia Press (Southern Anthropological Society Proceedings no. 34).

[7] Shandy, Dianna. 2003. "New Americans: The Road to Refugee Resettlement," *Conformity and Conflict: Readings in Cultural Anthropology* 11th ed., ed. James Spradley and David W. McCurdy (pp. 290–99). Boston: Allyn & Bacon.

Site Selection and Other Practical Considerations

Units of Analysis

One way to describe "the field" in which an ethnographer conducts research is to call it a *unit of analysis*. For our purposes in this introduction to ethnographic research, and because ethnographers in general are interested in the beliefs and behaviors of people in groups, we can say that the units of analysis in which we are most interested are sites like cities, neighborhoods, families, corporations, school districts (or even specific schools), health care agencies, and so forth. In order to be a workable unit of ethnographic analysis, the site should somehow be *countable*, *measurable*, and/or *describable*. "People who download music from the Internet" may sound like an interesting phenomenon for study, but it is certainly not something that easily fits as a "unit of analysis." One can certainly describe a particular behavior that characterizes such people (and that conceivably defines them as a "group"), but it is not a group that can in any reasonable way be counted or measured, partly because the activity is often covert and some people will not want to identify themselves as participating, and partly because participation, even if acknowledged, is a transitory thing—people do it, then don't do it, and then pick it up again as the fancy takes them, on no particular or regular schedule.

For these reasons, it is also helpful, particularly for the beginner, to choose a site that is *locatable*. In traditional ethnography, "location" almost always meant some recognizable physical space. But nowadays we recognize that real communities that are countable, measurable, describable units of analysis can be located in virtual space as well. So whether the site is bounded by conventional geography or by affiliation with, say, an Internet chat room, it is important that the researcher be readily able to find the people he or she wants to study. "People who don't floss after meals" is thus not a promising unit of analysis (even though such people might represent an interesting and important public health issue) since they have no reason to advertise their presence, nor do we have any reason to expect that they typically make common cause with each other (although in this day and age one would not necessarily want to rule out the possibility of a "We Hate to Floss" Web site somewhere out there).

The question of location also implies that a workable unit of analysis is somehow *bounded*. That is, it must be discernibly different from other groups and must not be so inclusive that it becomes unwieldy from sheer numbers. "Citizens of the United States" are certainly discernible as a group, but one would not want to construct an ethnography encompassing them all. (Survey research could work with a statistically representative sample of them, but that would not be ethnographic methodology.) On the other hand, "people licensed to drive" is too vague a criterion; while it might be a meaningful descriptor as part of a larger set of criteria, in and of itself it applies to a group that is far too heterogeneous to make a useful unit of analysis.

Some potential study sites are "naturally" bounded in the sense that the members have already decided that they form a meaningful group (e.g., Native Americans who live on a local reservation, people who attend a certain church, people who regularly post to a chat room for fans of a popular music group). Other sites are bounded because the researcher needs to set manageable limits (e.g., a study of the dietary patterns of people who eat at fast-food restaurants might have to be limited, at least in a preliminary study, to patrons of a single genre of franchise—burger, pizza, fried chicken, etc.—since otherwise the field is far too large to be studied efficiently).

Selection Criteria

Now that we have a basic working definition of a unit of analysis suitable for ethnographic study, we face the problem of choosing one in which we can actually conduct some research. There are three basic criteria that we need to take into account. First, there are *logistical criteria*, which may well be the most important for the small-scale projects in this book. In effect, we select a unit of analysis that is close by. We should also ask whether the group is one in which we can be a participant-observer without running up expenditures that outstrip our budget. It is also necessary to determine whether the unit of analysis is one that can be meaningfully studied by a single researcher, or if it is sufficiently large and complex to require the attention of a coordinated team. Can the group be dealt with in a time-efficient manner? Are there any potential barriers to entry (e.g., legal requirements)? All of these are logistical questions that will determine where you might want to do ethnographic work. For all these reasons, do not overlook your campus itself as a suitable setting for the exercises suggested in this book. The campus is likely to be an interestingly diverse set of linked communities in which access and other logistical considerations can be dealt with in a relatively easy way.

Also important are *definitional* and *conceptual* criteria. The former include the ways in which the group can be bounded ("people involved in the presidential election campaign" may be restricted to just those who work at campaign headquarters, rather than everyone who attends public rallies). Conceptual criteria include questions of "saturation"—in effect, are there sufficient numbers of people in the unit to make the study worthwhile? For example, you might be interested in how Hispanic high school students respond to college prep programs, but if the school you were thinking of working in has only two Hispanics out of a student body of 500, you're not likely to be able to answer your question. You would therefore continue looking until you found a school with a higher concentration (or saturation) of the kinds of people you are most interested in studying.

One aspect of site selection that is not necessarily a concern for ethnographers is the matter of *sampling*, which is a statistical process that insures that the unit(s) of analysis actually represents the beliefs or behaviors under study. For example, if one were interested in surveying general student opinions about people with mental retardation, one would have to make sure to sample respondents from many different constituencies on campus; it would be a questionable study at best if one limited one's survey to students majoring in special education. On the other hand, it would certainly be permissible to choose a unit of analysis that is representative only of itself (conducting, for example, an ethnographic case study of what working with people with mental disabilities has meant to those who have chosen a career in special education). Ethnographers are, indeed, often drawn to specialized, marginalized, or otherwise atypical groups who might otherwise be left out of consideration. But it is imperative that they identify a fringe community as such and not try to pass it off as somehow representative of wider society.

Some Practical Considerations

Before heading into the field to conduct ethnographic research, a student should conduct a basic inventory:

- ▲ Do I need any special permissions to enter this community, and if so, have I obtained all necessary clearances?
- ▲ Will I need any supplies to carry out my research (pads, pens, maps, index cards)?
- ▲ Will I need any special equipment to carry out my research (camera? video recorder? audio recorder? laptop computer? batteries?), and if so, do I have everything in good working order?
- ▲ Do I need to make arrangements for renting a place to live or an office to work out of?
- ▲ Do I have the kind of clothes and accessories that are considered appropriate and proper in this community?
- ▲ Do I need to make any special arrangements regarding transportation? (Where do I park my car? Can I take the bus, and if so, can I get a bus pass? Can I carpool? Is the site within walking distance?)

First Contact

Perhaps the most frightening aspect of doing ethnography is making the initial contact in the study community. It is sometimes possible (even desirable) for an ethnographer simply to enter the field "cold" and see who is available and who will take an interest in participating. I do not, however, advise this as a strategy for the short-term exercises in this book. You will be better served by having some advance preparation, as this precaution will lessen your anxiety (the very common "Suppose nobody talks to me?" nightmare of every ethnographer). Your instructor may be able to make some introductions for you in communities he or she has studied. Or you may be able to identify and get in touch with other *gatekeepers* (people who control access to a community). Do be cautious in this regard, however, as some people who put themselves forward as holding the keys to a community are not as well regarded by other members as they might think they are. If the site is a formal agency or institution like a school, hospital, day-care center, or recreational complex, you can be confident that there are people in obvious positions of authority who are the ones to consent to your presence and who will introduce you to the others. (You may, however, want to be cautious about giving the impression that you are nothing but a tool of "the boss" sent to spy on everyone else.) But if the site is an informal one, try to think of the kind of people who might be respected and influential. They may be the ones you would want to get to know first since they can become your guides to the rest of the community. Depending on the nature of the community, such people might be clergy, shopkeepers, social workers, political leaders, or well-known artists. A bit of investigation prior to actually entering the community will pay off in the end. In any case, you will not want to spend your entire field study hovering in the shadows of your first contact, but your ability to build rapport with everyone else will be greatly enhanced if you have chosen a good introducer.

Some Personal Considerations

One widely used textbook on ethnographic methods[1] lists several characteristics that are said to typify the "good" ethnographer. Such a person is:

▲ adventurous (observant and always alert to new possibilities)

▲ resourceful (able to get past mistakes or ideas that just don't pan out and try something different)

▲ enthusiastic (about the project and about meeting and dealing with the people in the community)

▲ self-motivated (since it is your interest that has taken you into this community, you can't rely on the people being a source of uncritical encouragement)

▲ trustworthy (since it is impossible to build rapport with people who think you are dishonest or even unacceptably eccentric)

▲ risk-taking (not being heedless and reckless, but being able to leave one's familiar "comfort zone" when the situation calls for it)

▲ curious (not being so wedded to a preset research agenda that one fails to follow up interesting leads; also refers to the ability and willingness to ask the sorts of probing questions that yield the most interesting information)

▲ sociable (works and interacts well with others)

▲ able to think conceptually (so as to be able to see the "big picture" and not get bogged down in a welter of details)

▲ culturally sensitive (able to recognize and respectfully deal with beliefs or behaviors different from one's own)

It should be obvious that this list represents a most lofty ideal—rare is the ethnographer who would earn a perfect score on this checklist. Even people with extensive backgrounds as researchers know that they fall short in one way or another. But the point is to be honest with oneself. Ask yourself: What am I good at? What things do I need to work on? How can I put myself in situations that maximize my strengths and minimize my weaknesses? Don't by any means count yourself a failure if you're not as "adventurous" or as adept at "conceptual thinking" as your classmate, and don't think that the game is up if your "enthusiasm" occasionally flags. It is quite normal for field workers to feel that they are not entirely up to the task; but if you keep your best qualities in mind and nurture them as they apply to your research project, then you will almost certainly come up with an interesting and useful result.

KEY TERMS

Be sure you can define and explain the importance of the following terms:

◆ gatekeepers   ◆ unit of analysis

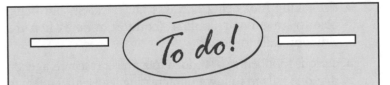

1. Before you try the more substantive exercises in the following chapters, conduct a personal inventory of your qualities as a potential ethnographer. (You need not show this inventory to anyone in the class, or even to your instructor. It is purely for your own information. As noted in chapter 1, the ethnographer is always his or her own main research instrument; the better you know yourself, the more effective you will be in using that instrument to do good research.) You may begin with the list in this chapter. What are your strong points? What are your weak points? How can you nurture your strengths and improve on your weaknesses? Thinking back to some of the comments made in chapter 1, what are some of the factors about yourself that you *cannot* change (your gender, racial or ethnic group, age category) that might bear on your ability to function as an ethnographer? How can you make sure to select a research site in which such factors will not be problematic?

2. Throughout this class, keep a *private* journal in which you record activities (in class, in conversations with your classmates, in the field) and also your reactions to them. Since this journal will not be shared with anyone *unless you choose to do so*, please be as honest as possible in documenting not only what you do this semester, but also how you feel as you do it. At the end of the semester go back to your journal to see if/how you have changed. (It should be noted that an ethnographer's journal can also serve a practical purpose in support of research, as it can often provide the context in which something you have recorded in your field notes originally occurred.)

3. Devise a plan for collecting the notes you make in the field, and for accessing them later on when you are writing a final report. If your instructor has a favored system that he or she wants you to follow, be sure you understand it and are able to use it before you begin the exercises. If not, come

up with something that makes sense to you. You may be comfortable using a computer to keep and index your notes. Or you may prefer more traditional methods such as index cards or loose-leaf notebooks. The important thing is that it is a system that works for *you*. You can do the most wonderful fieldwork, but if your notes are haphazard and you can't easily locate specific information when you need it, it will all be for naught.

4. Select a site at which you will be conducting your actual ethnographic projects. Keep in mind all the various selection criteria outlined in this chapter. Make sure that your instructor is aware of and approves your choice.

NOTE

[1] LeCompte, Margaret D. and Jean J. Schensul. 1999. *Designing and Conducting Ethnographic Research*. Walnut Creek, CA: AltaMira Press.

Ethnographic Observation

Getting Started

The first of the key techniques in ethnographic research is *observation*. We must always keep in mind that ethnography is a process by which a researcher inserts himself or herself into the everyday lives of those whose beliefs and behaviors are to be studied. But even when that insertion is facilitated by introductions from people known and respected in the community, the researcher is likely to be at something of a loss for a while: so much is going on that it is hard to know where to begin. *What*, after all, should be observed, and *how* does useful observation take place?

We might think that observation is hardly a research technique at all since it's something we do all the time quite naturally. But in fact it is *not* as natural a process as it might seem.

If we consider all the myriad things that go on in even the most mundane situations, we can see that we would rapidly reach sensory overload if we paid equal attention to everything. In fact, we are able to get through our own everyday lives in our own cultures only because we have developed habits of *non*observation. That is, as we grow up and gain familiarity with our own culture, we gradually learn all of the many things we can take for granted and that we don't need to be concerned with. But when we are in a new situation, as in "the field" for a research project, at first we can't always be sure we are picking up all the right cues. We can't assume that we know what we can safely ignore. Our anthropological training might lead us to guess that the cues that work in our own culture probably won't be as useful to us in different settings (even ones that seem superficially similar). But then, what do we do?

A standard textbook definition of *observation* tells us simply that it is that which "can be seen through the eyes of the ethnographer."[1] I'm afraid that this definition isn't very helpful, since we are still very likely to be overwhelmed by all that we can see through our eyes. Moreover, we do not learn about the world around us only through our eyes. We "observe" using all our senses, and so we must be concerned with everything the ethnographer can *perceive* through any or all of his/her five senses. I think we can intuit that the "eyes" through which an experienced ethnographer "sees" are somehow different from the "eyes" that get us through everyday life. So until we have a better grasp of the local culture (which provides the "filters" that help us know which things can be ignored), we must first of all rely on our formative theory. Don't let this term scare you off if you think that "theory" is only for the most advanced scholars. In fact, a theory is simply a way to discern patterns in data and to come up with an explanation for why those patterns exist. A *formative theory* is nothing more than the explanatory framework that guides one in the initial approach to a new setting. It may well be modified as the research progresses, but it is a useful way to begin sorting through the mass of observed detail.

The mere fact that you have chosen one setting over another in order to do your fieldwork—even small-scale projects like the ones in this book—is an operation of formative theory. To be sure, some of your selective criteria are purely pragmatic (nearness to campus, friendly gatekeepers willing to introduce you to the community, etc.). But others must surely reflect your own concerns. Are you particularly interested in education? religion? the arts? law enforcement? recreational activities? Expressing such an interest does not mean that you think all other aspects of life in the community are unimportant; just that you think that the one you are drawn to is a reasonable microcosm of the larger whole. So your perception of what does and does not constitute a reasonable microcosm is already an important element in your formative theory. For example, if you think that modern American culture is defined by its enthusiasm for pop culture, then you would probably not select an Amish farming village as the site of your study, no matter how friendly the people might be. In any case, once you have decided on a focus for your study, you can begin to detect patterns in terms of those things that *seem* to have a direct relationship to that pattern. (Your preliminary conclusions may well evolve over the course of the project, but that shouldn't dissuade you from working with them as an initial set of guidelines.)

In my study of deinstitutionalized adults with mental disabilities, for example, I began with the formative theory that people who were relatively secure in their knowledge of basic survival skills would do better out in the community (i.e., would be less likely to seek "normal" benefactors to help them make decisions) than those lacking in self-confidence. So I began by studying people at agencies that provided various kinds of skills training to find out more about what kinds of things people with mental disabilities could learn and how they assimilated their lessons. Later in the project I realized that learning does not take place only in formal training institutions—all of the settings in which peer interaction takes place are important as well—but my choice of training facilities was a good way to start, or else I could have spent many fruitless months simply wandering around, following people at random.

Once you have narrowed your observational focus by means of even the most general formative theory, you can begin the actual process of observation. I want to stress two important points at this stage of the game.

▲ "Observation" may be based on what the ethnographer can see, but what is seen does not become data until it is somehow recorded in such a way that it can be retrieved. In other words, don't try to rely on your memory to reconstruct patterns as you go along. Make sure you can back up your statement of such patterns with clearly recorded information.

▲ Even if you are working in a setting that is relatively familiar to you (and the audience for your report), pretend at the outset that you are recording information about a truly exotic setting about which little, if anything, can be taken for granted. Don't worry that you are noting lots of detail; you will gradually stop doing so once you become more familiar with the setting. But at first it is better to assume that everything you see in your selected setting is potentially relevant.

Your first observational notes should be guided by the traditional objective questions typical of journalism: who is involved (even if you don't yet know people by name, you can describe them generically—e.g., middle-aged white woman with two children)? What happened? Where did it happen? When did it happen? (Later, as you gain familiarity, you can deal with more complex matters, such as *why* it happened.) Your notes should be supplemented, whenever possible, by visual aids (photos, sketches, maps) so that you can locate these objective facts in a definable space.

At the outset, try to keep your field notes as free as possible from interpretation. Don't write, for example, "The people were carried away with religious fervor at the church service." Rather, write, "People were singing, shouting, and dancing during the church service." Don't write, "The hospital room was cheerful." Rather, write, "The hospital room was painted yellow and was decorated with flowers and balloons." Don't write, "The students were frustrated with the teacher's explanation," but rather, "The students were fidgeting and kept glancing at one another." Your personal interpretations can (and should) be recorded in your journal, but not in your field notes.

Try to keep the following points in mind as you write your field notes.

▲ Try to record as many exact quotes as possible, so as to give the flavor of how the participants are reacting.

▲ Use pseudonyms or other codes to identify participants. You may end up using their real names in the final report *if* that agreement is part of the signed informed consent form, but keep the notes themselves as anonymous as possible since they are still "raw" data and subject to possible misinterpretation should some unauthorized person read them.

▲ Make sure that the notes follow the sequence of events as carefully as possible. You can get fancy in your final report, but the notes are not the place for literary devices like flashbacks, flash-forwards, anticipations, etc.

▲ Make sure that each notation is carefully dated.

▲ Make sure that each notation carries some indication of your own devising that tells you which category of information it is to be filed under for future reference.

Types of Observation

Unobtrusive Observation

Unobtrusive observations are those made with a minimum of researcher participation. Some classic studies in *proxemics* (how people use physical space)[2] and *kinesics* (how people convey meaning through "body language")[3] were conducted in this way. In these cases, the researchers stationed themselves in some busy public place (e.g., an airport waiting area, a library reading room, a hospital emergency room) and took notes on the behaviors of interest without interacting with anyone and without (if at all possible) attracting any attention. Ethnography, as we have been using the term in this book, generally involves more extensive researcher participation, but this sort of unobtrusive observation may well be a good way to get started, particularly if you are initially shy about meeting people.

Unobtrusive observation is often ***structured observation***, which means that a very precise format for recording data is used. For example, in a proxemic study, there may be an outline drawing of the hospital ER, with all of its fixed landmarks (doors, windows, chairs, tables, curtained areas, reception desks, etc.) clearly indicated. Multiple copies of the drawing can be made, and then at preset intervals (e.g., every half hour) the researcher records who is sitting where and doing what in relation to those fixed points in the space of the setting. In this way, one can gain a sense of space usage as it flows over time. Another application of such strictly structured data recording comes when multiple researchers are simultaneously observing similar, but different, settings. For example, a team of researchers might fan out to six different ERs around the city. Using the same kinds of drawings and a predetermined set of symbols (ways to represent males, females, children, doctors, patients, nurses, etc.), all recorded at the predetermined time intervals, the team can make reasonably sure that they will have truly comparable data. The classic work of comparative structured observation is the "six cultures" study. Ethnographers conducted fieldwork in six different parts of the world. They were all interested in practices related to child rearing, and all used the same format for observing and recording data.[4]

Participant Observation

More typical of ethnography is true participant observation. In such cases, the researcher is someone already familiar to the people in the study group. The researcher's purposes are generally known (i.e., to collect information about such and such a topic). And the researcher is actively doing something at the same time everyone else is doing it—he or she is not simply sitting in a corner taking notes. Participant observation does indeed raise some tricky questions about note taking since it is not possible to note things as they happen (as in unobtrusive research). It is usually not feasible (and might even be considered offensive in some settings) to stop participating in the action in order to type something on your laptop or scribble something in your notebook. So despite the earlier warning about not relying on your memory, sometimes the circumstances of participant observation require you to wait until after the event in order to record your notes. But by all means be sure you do so at the earliest possible moment following the event.

Participant observation is usually ***unstructured observation***. Since the researcher is immersed in the flow of events as they are unfolding, it is rarely feasible to use the sort of preplanned recording forms noted above—there are too many unanticipated variables at play. Moreover, for reasons suggested above, it is rarely possible to stop to make notes according to a timed schedule during the course of participant observation. For this reason, participant observation is usually not a good choice if one's research design calls for controlled comparisons. Because participant observation relies on the specific qualities and attributes of the researcher, each piece of unstructured observation will be unique.

KEY TERMS

Be sure you can define and explain the importance of the following terms:

- ◆ formative theory
- ◆ kinesics
- ◆ participant observation
- ◆ proxemics

- ◆ structured observation
- ◆ unobtrusive observation
- ◆ unstructured observation

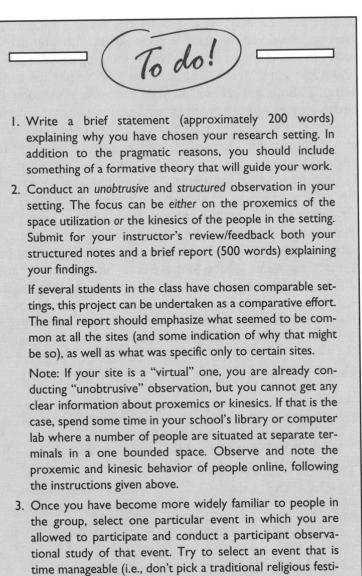

_To do!_

1. Write a brief statement (approximately 200 words) explaining why you have chosen your research setting. In addition to the pragmatic reasons, you should include something of a formative theory that will guide your work.

2. Conduct an _unobtrusive_ and _structured_ observation in your setting. The focus can be _either_ on the proxemics of the space utilization _or_ the kinesics of the people in the setting. Submit for your instructor's review/feedback both your structured notes and a brief report (500 words) explaining your findings.

   If several students in the class have chosen comparable settings, this project can be undertaken as a comparative effort. The final report should emphasize what seemed to be common at all the sites (and some indication of why that might be so), as well as what was specific only to certain sites.

   Note: If your site is a "virtual" one, you are already conducting "unobtrusive" observation, but you cannot get any clear information about proxemics or kinesics. If that is the case, spend some time in your school's library or computer lab where a number of people are situated at separate terminals in a one bounded space. Observe and note the proxemic and kinesic behavior of people online, following the instructions given above.

3. Once you have become more widely familiar to people in the group, select one particular event in which you are allowed to participate and conduct a participant observational study of that event. Try to select an event that is time manageable (i.e., don't pick a traditional religious festival that lasts for eight days) and that unfolds only in one place. Submit for your instructor's review/feedback both your notes and a brief report (500 words) explaining your findings. Remember, at this point, try to steer clear of too many interpretations—allow the event as you have recorded it to speak for itself as much as possible. And

even if you select an event that you have reason to believe will be familiar to most people (e.g., a football game), treat it as if you were describing it to someone who knows little about it or its place in the culture.

Several students might be able to select comparable events at comparable sites. While they will not be using a structured methodology as in the previous project, they will still be able to compare/contrast their experiences in a common report, focusing on what role the students think their various personal qualities may have played in shaping what they observed.

NOTES

[1] Schensul, Stephen L., Jean J. Schensul, and Margaret D. LeCompte. 1999. *Essential Ethnographic Methods.* Walnut Creek, CA: AltaMira Press.

[2] Hall, Edward T. 1959. *The Silent Language.* New York: Doubleday.

[3] Birdwhistell, Ray. 1952. *Introduction to Kinesics: An Annotation System for Analysis of Body Motion and Gesture.* Washington, DC: Department of State, Foreign Service Institute.

[4] Whiting, John W., Irvin L. Child, and William W. Lambert. 1966. *Field Guide for the Study of Socialization.* New York: Wiley.

Ethnographic Interviewing

In the previous chapter we noted that there is a tendency to think that observation is a natural, and hence easily accomplished, feat. But we also saw that observation as it is conducted by an ethnographic researcher involves considerably more than what it takes to be aware of one's surroundings on an everyday basis. The same temptation also applies to the second major research tool—interviewing. Interviewing may seem on the surface to be like ordinary conversation. We also see examples of professional interviewing all the time on TV so it doesn't seem all that mysterious. And everyone is familiar with surveys, questionnaires, and polls. But while ethnographic interviewing does indeed have a conversational component, it is as different from ordinary conversation as ethnographic observation (with its detailed note-taking and pattern-discerning features) is different from ordinary awareness. The sorts of interviews we see on TV usually feature politicians seeking support or celebrities pitching their latest movies, CDs, or books; their statements are programmed and it is the rare interviewer who even tries to interject anything resembling a truly probing question. It should also be obvious that a participant-observer immersed in the community under study would have to go beyond simply asking a series of predetermined survey questions. Therefore, interviewing in service to ethnographic research must be substantially different from the more familiar ways of conducting an interview.

Types of Ethnographic Interviews

The Exploratory Interview

The *exploratory interview* is perhaps the most typical of all ethnographic methods, tied as it is to the overall strategy of participant observation. Its basic purpose is to probe issues of concern that the researcher believes to be important to the study but about which little is known. The identification of an issue of concern may come from a prior formative theory, or it may arise out of increased understanding of the people in the community and their culture as a result of ongoing interaction with them.

The exploratory interview is often described as an *in-depth interviewing* technique because the topic is dealt with in great detail so as to deepen the researcher's understanding of that topic. It may also be described as an *open-ended interview* because the interviewer avoids "forced-choice," yes-or-no questions in favor of those that lend themselves to extended narrative responses and that are open to any and all relevant responses.

In sum, an exploratory interview:

▲ explores previously undefined aspects of the formative theory (explanatory model)

▲ identifies new aspects of the situation or new patterns within it

▲ breaks down patterns into component factors

- ▲ obtains contextualizing information about the background of the setting and its people
- ▲ contributes to building rapport between the researcher and the people in the community

Two forms of the exploratory ethnographic interview that I have used extensively in my own research are the life history[1] and the oral history.[2] A *life history* is a record of an individual person's life story; the interviewee may be chosen *either* because he or she is seen as a typical or representative figure in his or her community (such that his or her life story is a kind of microcosm of the larger culture) *or* because he or she is an extraordinary figure who stands for the ideals or aspirations of the common folk. An *oral history*, by contrast, is concerned with one specific event in the history of a community; the people interviewed have direct knowledge of the event, and they speak only of that event and not about everything else that has ever happened to them.

When conducting an exploratory interview, the researcher must:

- ▲ remember how the specific topic of the interview relates to and illuminates the larger themes of the study;
- ▲ decide whether the person being interviewed is staying on topic and, if not, how to be diplomatic in steering the conversation back in the right direction (it is important to note that sometimes what seems like a digression is something of real importance to the person being interviewed, so the ethnographer must never be too hasty in getting back to his or her own agenda);
- ▲ probe for the meaning of unfamiliar terms and clarify such potentially confusing matters as dates, spelling of names, and chronologies.

It is therefore very important that the ethnographic interviewer be constantly alert and attentive to what the interviewee is saying. (In normal conversation, by contrast, it is possible for our attention to wander, much as in everyday observation we can afford to take much for granted.) Paying attention to the person you are interviewing does *not* mean that you provide unblinking eye contact, which can be easily interpreted as creepy. But there are acceptable ways to keep focus; for example, interjecting such phrases as, "Oh, I see," or "That's a really interesting point," or even that old standby, "Hmmm. . . ."

It is also important to keep in mind that the ethnographic interview is something like a conversation between friends; it is not the impersonal interrogation of a "subject." Modern day ethnographers often refer to the people they interview as their "collaborators" since the interview is really a joint production of the researcher and the storyteller. Therefore, try to set a time and place for the interview that is comfortable and convenient for you both. Begin with some icebreaking chitchat (unless the person you are interviewing tells you he or she is very busy and expects you to get right down to business). Do not be shy about expressing your own opinions or sharing stories about experiences you may have had that bear on what the person is talking about. Don't hijack the conversation with your own narrative, of course, but conversation does imply give and take. While you should not become confrontational or argumentative, don't be afraid to say something that contradicts what the interviewee has said if you believe strongly in that position. Keep in mind that certain kinds of interviews, especially perhaps life histories and oral histories, can bring up sad and/or painful memories—be prepared to deal with an interviewee who begins to cry or give other indications of being upset. It might be tactful for you to suggest a break, perhaps to get some coffee, and then get back to the interview when the person has composed himself or herself.

Perhaps most important, know when to stop. Don't think that an interview has to be of a certain length in order to be valid. Be alert to the cues that your interviewee will use to let you know that he or she has had enough (e.g., the information is getting repetitive; the person starts to fidget and look at his or her watch; the person starts to talk about other obligations— "Oh, I've really got to get dinner in the oven by the time the kids come home from school"). If you really think there are more things to talk about, suggest a follow-up session at a later date rather than force the person to sit there when it is clear he or she would rather be somewhere else. Don't, however, be thrown by pauses or even fairly long silences. Sometimes people need time to think and reflect. Be sure you can tell the difference between a pause that indicates thoughtful introspection from one that indicates boredom or lack of knowledge.

One very common pitfall when conducting interviews is picking the wrong person. Most people are flattered to be asked to share their stories—*if* they are being asked to talk about something they know a lot about. Don't ask someone to sit for an interview on a topic about which he or she knows little just because he or she is a nice person whom you want to spend some time with. Ethnographers sometimes speak of their **key informants**—those who are particularly knowledgeable and who can be counted on to serve as authoritative guides to certain aspects of the local culture. Not everyone in the community is going to be equally knowledgeable and you will save yourself considerable time and effort if you select your interviewees wisely.

As you prepare for the interview, come up with a set of basic questions that you want to deal with. These should by no means be treated as if they formed a survey questionnaire, to be asked one-by-one in an interrogatory manner. Indeed, the conversation may drift around these topics in no particular order. Don't be concerned if this happens; as long as everything you think is important has been covered, don't worry that the narrative isn't coming out in the orderly fashion you envisioned. You can keep your list of questions in a notebook that is handy for you to glance at, but that isn't a major feature of your interview. If it turns out that something of importance isn't getting covered, you can remind yourself of it and try diplomatically to steer the conversation around to it. In the case of life history and oral history, don't jump to the conclusion that the stories have to be told in absolute chronological order. People's memories don't necessarily work that way—sometimes they work by *allusion*, one idea sparking others in a nonlinear fashion. If for some reason it is important for the final narrative to take a strictly chronological form, then it can be achieved in the final editing process; but do not force your interviewee to tell the story that way if he or she does not seem so inclined.

The matter of your notebook raises another significant point. It is standard practice for ethnographic interviews to be recorded on audiotape. Most people are familiar with this technology and do not find it distracting (although you might want to be prepared to demonstrate it and let someone "play" with it if you encounter people to whom it is all new); on the other hand, taking notes by hand *is* distracting because it forces you to break eye contact far too often. And unless you are a whiz with shorthand (and very few of us are these days) there's no way you can capture the entire conversation in writing. So keep the notebook for the occasional note or reminder, not as the place where the entire interview is recorded. If the interview concerns a topic with a highly visual component (e.g., if you are interviewing an artist about his or her creations) you might want to consider videotaping the interview. But audiotape is the medium of preference. It is inexpensive and readily available. Your instructor can let you know if there is equipment available to borrow at your school in case you do not have any of your own. If you do have to or want to go out and buy something, don't feel you need to go top-of-the-line; unless your interview requires the recording of very fine sonic detail (e.g., you are interviewing a singer), the sort of recorder and tape cassette available at any retail store should be fine. Just make sure that you know how to use the recorder and that it is in proper working order before you set out for your interview. And be sure you have enough tape and sufficient batteries (you might be interviewing someone in a park and cannot rely on plugging it into a wall outlet) to see you through the interview. Record a "header" at the beginning of each tape ("This is John Doe interviewing Jane Smith on May 31, 2004, at Battery Park"); doing so is not only a way to keep track of what's on a tape just in case you forget to label it—it is also a way to make sure the machine is actually recording before you begin the interview itself. Go ahead and record the icebreaking chitchat because turning on the machine later sends the wrong message: all that conversational stuff was unimportant, and now we really begin. Above all, don't panic if disaster strikes (e.g., the tape gets hopelessly snarled, the batteries fail suddenly, you have forgotten to turn on the machine before commencing the interview). Yes, you will have lost valuable information, but if you have chosen your interviewee well, he or she will almost certainly be willing to do it all again at another time.

Ethnographic interviewing can result in a very large body of data that are not as easily summarized as numerical information. There is thus always a question as to what to do with the tapes once the interview is recorded. Experienced ethnographers are divided on this issue. Some insist that it is absolutely necessary to have full written transcriptions of every recorded interview; their analysis works from the written transcriptions rather than from the tapes themselves. (This approach is also necessitated when one uses one of the increasingly popular software programs designed for the analysis of narrative data.) But others prefer to work from selected indexes of the tapes and to retrieve specific pieces of the spoken word on an as-needed basis. For the limited projects in this book, you will not have to worry about this problem, as you will not be generating more than a few cassettes. Simply for the practice of doing so, therefore, you should do complete transcripts of all your tapes—even though in the pursuit of future research you think you may choose to do otherwise.

In sum, the exploratory interview only seems unstructured and loose at first glance. In truth, it requires a great deal of patience, persistence, alertness, logical thinking, and excellent communication skills.

The Semi-Structured Interview

Participant-observers collect a large portion of their information through the exploratory interviews discussed above. Sometimes, however, those interviews yield insights that seem to require very precise double-checking. In such circumstances, it is possible to devise a *semi-structured interview* (sometimes referred to as a focused interview), which consists of predetermined questions related to a very specific topic and is administered to a representative sample of respondents (not just the most interested key informants) to confirm (or reject) ideas raised by the exploratory interview. The semi-structured interview might also be used to identify variables that can only be further tested by being built into a fully quantified survey instrument administered to a broad sample. It therefore bridges the gap between purely qualitative ethnographic research and purely quantitative hypothesis-testing research. For example, a team of researchers led by Stephen Schensul learned from prior ethnographic research that the risk of contracting AIDS varies significantly depending on the kinds of influences a person's family, work environment, and peer groups exert on his/her behavior. Semi-structured interviews were conducted based on questions related to each of these areas of social life in order to get a clearer idea of how these factors relate to one another.[3] In my own research with deinstitutionalized adults, my exploratory interviews yielded insights into their concerns about sexuality, but it was necessary to see how widely (if at all) such concerns were shared by a larger sample of clients at relevant agencies. My initial group of interviewees was asked to speak freely about their entire lives (exploratory interviews); the second group was asked specifically about sexuality (semi-structured interviews).

Keep the following points in mind when constructing questions for a semi-structured interview.

▲ Use language that is understandable to all respondents (as opposed to words or phrases that might be known only to specialists like your initial key informant).

▲ Questions should be brief; avoid confusing compound questions by asking only one thing at a time.

▲ Avoid "leading questions" (those that imply the answer you expect to get—e.g., do not say, "It must have been tough growing up during the Depression, right?" but rather, "What was it like growing up during the Depression?").

▲ Avoid questions that may put ideas into the heads of respondents (e.g., do not say, "Are you ever afraid that your views on school busing will lead people to think you're a racist?" but rather, "How do you think people respond to your views on busing?").

▲ Avoid negatively worded questions (e.g., do not say, "Don't you think abortion is wrong?" but rather, "What do you think about abortion?").

▲ Avoid questions that require respondents to rank-order responses (since such questions require somewhat complicated explanations that can be confusing and time-consuming).

▲ Do not ask questions that can be answered "yes" or "no" when you really need a more descriptive response.

▲ Be sensitive to the cultural nuances of questions (e.g., in some cultures, women will be embarrassed and offended if asked questions about sexual matters by a male interviewer).

As noted above, we need not be concerned with the ordering of questions in an exploratory interview, but question ordering is a matter of some concern in semi-structured interviews. A few general points can be addressed in this regard.

▲ Ask questions in temporal sequence (going from earlier events to more recent ones).

▲ Ask questions in ascending order of complexity (start with the simple and work your way up to the complex).

▲ Ask questions on a single topic together before going on to another topic.

▲ Ask questions beginning with the most concrete and working up to the most abstract.

▲ Ask questions beginning with those least likely to be perceived as threatening or sensitive and work up to those that might pose some difficulty.

KEY TERMS

Be sure you can define and explain the importance of the following terms:

- ◆ exploratory interview
- ◆ in-depth interview
- ◆ key informant
- ◆ life history
- ◆ open-ended interview
- ◆ oral history
- ◆ semi-structured interview

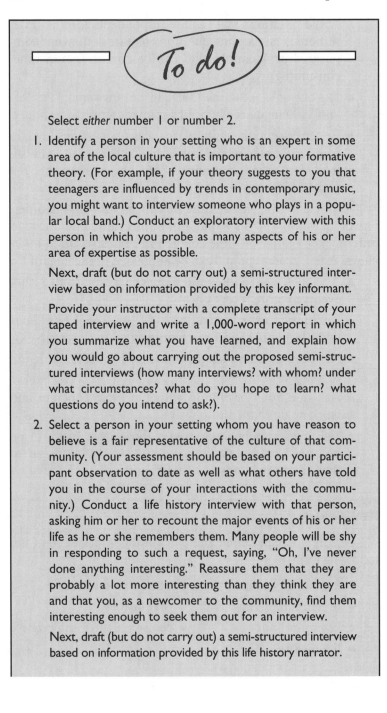

To do!

Select *either* number 1 or number 2.

1. Identify a person in your setting who is an expert in some area of the local culture that is important to your formative theory. (For example, if your theory suggests to you that teenagers are influenced by trends in contemporary music, you might want to interview someone who plays in a popular local band.) Conduct an exploratory interview with this person in which you probe as many aspects of his or her area of expertise as possible.

   Next, draft (but do not carry out) a semi-structured interview based on information provided by this key informant.

   Provide your instructor with a complete transcript of your taped interview and write a 1,000-word report in which you summarize what you have learned, and explain how you would go about carrying out the proposed semi-structured interviews (how many interviews? with whom? under what circumstances? what do you hope to learn? what questions do you intend to ask?).

2. Select a person in your setting whom you have reason to believe is a fair representative of the culture of that community. (Your assessment should be based on your participant observation to date as well as what others have told you in the course of your interactions with the community.) Conduct a life history interview with that person, asking him or her to recount the major events of his or her life as he or she remembers them. Many people will be shy in responding to such a request, saying, "Oh, I've never done anything interesting." Reassure them that they are probably a lot more interesting than they think they are and that you, as a newcomer to the community, find them interesting enough to seek them out for an interview.

   Next, draft (but do not carry out) a semi-structured interview based on information provided by this life history narrator.

Provide your instructor with a complete transcript of your taped interview[4] and write a 1,000-word report in which you summarize what you have learned, and explain how you would go about carrying out the proposed semi-structured interviews (how many interviews? with whom? under what circumstances? what do you hope to learn? what questions do you intend to ask?).

3. Although students in the class will be working in different settings, they will all be doing research in the same general community (i.e., the same city or region surrounding the university campus). It is therefore probable that there will be an event of major importance that has affected people in all the different settings. For example, a common topic might be, "Responses to the Events of 9/11/01 in Our Community."

Each student should therefore conduct a few brief oral history interviews in his or her particular setting, as a contribution to a larger mosaic in which that event is recorded for the community as a whole.

With your instructor's guidance, you may want to create an oral history archive at your school where you can preserve these tapes (making sure, of course, that you have the respondents' signed permission to do so). If the tapes are thus preserved, it will not be necessary to make full transcriptions; an index will suffice as well as a plan for accessing those tapes should others want to listen to them. Provide your instructor with a 500-word summary of your findings.

NOTES

[1] Langness, L. L. and Gelya Frank. 1981. *Lives: An Anthropological Approach to Biography.* Novato, CA: Chandler and Sharp.

[2] Yow, Valerie. 1994. *Recording Oral History: A Practical Guide for Social Scientists.* Thousand Oaks, CA: Sage.

[3] Schensul, Stephen, et al. 1994. *Young Women, Work, and AIDS-related Risk Behavior.* Washington, DC: International Center for Research on Women.

[4] See Redfern-Vance, Nancy. 2002. "Analyzing Narrative Data," *Doing Cultural Anthropology,* ed. Michael V. Angrosino (pp. 45–62). Prospect Heights, IL: Waveland Press for some suggestions on transcribing narrative.

Ethnography and the Analysis of Archived Materials

When ethnographers speak of *archived materials*, they are referring to records stored for research, service, and other official or unofficial purposes by researchers, service agencies, and other groups. The data are stored in the formats in which they were collected, although in modern times some of them have been transferred to media such as microform or CD-ROM. In other words, archived materials are data originally collected for some purpose specific to the person or agency doing the collecting; those data, however, are now open to the researcher who is interested in seeing what they reveal about the history and culture of a given community. The analysis of archived materials is thus a necessary adjunct to the collection of firsthand data through observation and interviewing in the field.

For ethnographers, some of the most important types of archived material are:

- ▲ maps (both those produced by governments and those sketched by ordinary people for their own purposes)
- ▲ municipal, state, or other governmental records of births, marriages, real estate transactions, auto registrations, and property ownership
- ▲ church (or other religious body) records of births, marriages, baptisms
- ▲ census, tax, and voting lists
- ▲ records of human service agencies (e.g., clinics, welfare programs, schools)
- ▲ court proceedings and arrest records
- ▲ minutes of meetings of local groups
- ▲ copies of old newspapers, magazines, flyers, brochures
- ▲ collections of photos, letters, or other memorabilia, whether on public exhibit or held in private

Do not neglect formal museums, a very rich source of information. True, it has been collected and organized according to somebody else's plan, but it is there for you to draw on for your own purposes. Some museums are devoted specifically to artifacts that would traditionally be associated with the anthropological study of culture (e.g., those devoted to Native Americans or other ethnic groups). The anthropologist Serena Nanda describes viewing a collection housed in the African room of the American Museum of Natural History in New York City. She was intrigued by a carving of a slave ship that depicted an Englishman on the bow. This observation led her to a research project on non-Europeans' depictions of Europeans during the era of colonialism and slavery— research that took her ultimately to many other museum collections. Even museums that do not have an obvious ethnographic focus (e.g., those devoted to works of art, science, technology, or history) can tell us a lot, not only about the obvious subject matter of the displays but also about the perspectives of the people who put them together. In addition to large public museums, there are also smaller exhibit galleries associated with institutions such as schools, churches, local historical societies, hospitals, or other social agencies.[1]

Another form of archived data that might prove useful in ethnographic research are *secondary data*, information collected by other researchers for other purposes, but which can be re-analyzed for one's own purposes. The raw notes of some prior ethnographers are available at libraries or museums, and much ethnographic data from the past century have been compiled on ethnographic databases such as the *Atlas of World Cultures*, the *Standard Ethnographic Sample*, and the *Human Relations Area File;* your campus library may have these databases on hand. Of these three, the **Human Relations File** (HRAF) is probably the best known and most widely used. It includes information about 360 cultures and is the only one of the databases that currently provides full text. For example, if one were interested in "shamanism," one could look up passages from all the ethnographies written about cultures around the world in which shamanism is discussed. One can also use the HRAF to answer specific research questions: which are more common—male or female shamans?

Archival research is *nonreactive research* in the sense that the researcher is not in direct contact with those under study. This condition eliminates the possibility of the researcher unduly influencing the outcome of a field inquiry, although it has the disadvantage of eliminating the sense of personal familiarity with the material. For that reason, the use of archived materials should always be a process taken in tandem with other forms of ethnographic data collection unless circumstances are such that firsthand fieldwork is impossible. For example, during World War II a group of American anthropologists wanted to compile as much descriptive data as possible about the national cultures of the peoples involved in the war, both as allies and as enemies. In the case of the latter, it was clearly not feasible to go do firsthand ethnography in Germany or Japan and so portraits of those people were pulled together from a wide variety of archived materials (e.g., newspapers, magazines, movies, songs, works of fiction) that were readily available in the United States and Britain.[2]

Archived materials are also useful in that they support the analysis of cultural processes through time. An interdisciplinary group of faculty and students from my university collaborated on a project to reconstruct the history of a once-thriving African American neighborhood in Tampa, one that had been largely destroyed by "urban renewal" in the 1960s. The researchers studied all the sources outlined earlier in this chapter in order to document the impact of federal, state, and local urban renewal policy on the neighborhood and the ways in which community residents responded to the impending destruction of their neighborhood. The project concluded with a photo exhibit, a panel discussion, and a guided walking tour of the area.

Even something as apparently mundane as a collection of high school yearbooks can yield all sorts of fascinating data about everything from changing hairstyles to evolving conceptions of gender roles. Of course, we must always take such information with a grain or two of salt. A high school yearbook, for example, is usually produced under the auspices of a school administration that naturally has a vested interest in putting the best face possible on the school, its students and faculty, and its programs and activities. We cannot assume that a yearbook—or any such source—is telling us the whole story, or, at least, the story that we are most interested in learning about. In the absence of other data, however, it is far better than nothing at all. The activities of ordinary people do not always make the pages of the standard history texts; but to a surprising degree traces of their lives are recorded in all these bodies of data. Reconstruction of the lives and activities of "voiceless" people (minorities, women, people with disabilities, and others who have historically existed at the margins of mainstream society and whose experiences rarely made the "official" histories) has been aided immeasurably by the recovery of just this sort of archived material.[3] Many university and state archives contain oral history collections, sometimes devoted to particular topics (e.g., Native Americans, first settlers, immigrants). These collections (and the librarians who work with them) are good sources for how to do oral history research, but more pertinent to the topic of this chapter, they are sources of archived material that might illuminate contemporary research you are doing in the community.

One practical problem that researchers often encounter when using archived materials is that they may well be stored in haphazard ways in less than ideal situations. You may have to be prepared to spend hours sifting through bug-flecked, unindexed piles of dusty newspaper clippings before finding something you really need. Public records, as opposed to privately held collections, are usually in somewhat better shape, but they may be restricted in access. Even if they are not, we cannot count on the government doing a significantly better job of keeping tabs on everything it collects. (You may remember the amusing sequence in the film *Erin Brockovich* in which the crusading paralegal has to go to extraordinary lengths just to get to see a county's supposedly public water use documents, and then has to spend a huge amount of time trying to sort through the chaotic record-keeping "system" in order to get the information she needs to make her case.)

KEY TERMS

Be sure you can define and explain the importance of the following terms:

- ▲ archived materials
- ▲ nonreactive research
- ▲ Human Relations Area File
- ▲ secondary data

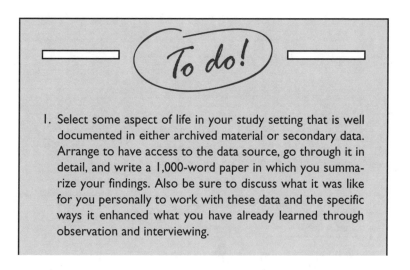

To do!

1. Select some aspect of life in your study setting that is well documented in either archived material or secondary data. Arrange to have access to the data source, go through it in detail, and write a 1,000-word paper in which you summarize your findings. Also be sure to discuss what it was like for you personally to work with these data and the specific ways it enhanced what you have already learned through observation and interviewing.

> Students working in different settings, but using a similar data source (e.g., newspaper clippings), should get together and submit a brief compare/contrast report about the pros and cons of this sort of ethnographic research.

Notes

[1] Stocking, George W., ed. 1985. *Objects and Others: Essays on Museums and Material Culture.* Madison: University of Wisconsin Press.

[2] Mead, Margaret and Rhoda Metraux, eds. 1953. *The Study of Culture at a Distance.* Chicago: University of Chicago Press.

[3] Lewis, Earl. 1996. "Connecting Memory, Self, and the Power of Place in African American Urban History," *The New African American Urban History*, ed. Kenneth W. Goings and Raymond A. Mohl (pp. 1–15). Thousand Oaks, CA: Sage.

Presenting
Your Findings

Having reached this point in the book, you have already
learned how to:

▲ identify a social setting that makes for a reasonable, feasible "unit of analysis" for ethnographic study;

▲ come up with a meaningful explanation (formative theory) of a useful and interesting aspect of culture that can
be effectively studied in that setting;

▲ conduct an honest review of your own strengths and
weaknesses as a researcher;

▲ devise a plan for keeping and retrieving notes from the
field;

▲ "see through the eyes of an ethnographer" by conducting both unobtrusive and participant observational
studies in your selected setting;

▲ ask probing questions that help people in your setting
reconstruct their histories and/or reflect on issues of
current concern;

▲ access and make sense of archived material pertinent to the history and/or current circumstances of your community and its people.

In other words, you have done everything that a "real" ethnographer must do in order to conduct research in the field and you have begun to practice the three skills most basic to collecting ethnographic data: observing, interviewing, and locating and analyzing archived materials. You have therefore taken some significant steps toward answering the question, "How do they know that?" You have, in effect, worked through the process of ethnography, and you have come up with an ethnographic product. You have looked at your chosen unit of analysis through at least three different lenses (i.e., you have practiced "triangulation" when honing in on your conclusions) in order to generate something approaching a comprehensive overview.

But one further process remains: the dissemination of the knowledge amassed in the course of research, which is your "To Do" for this chapter.

The purpose of research is to communicate information and insight to some larger audience; research data that stay locked up in the files of the researcher are of very limited use. Any researcher has several audiences to be concerned with. Students, of course, have a primary audience in their instructor and will need to present their findings in ways the latter finds most desirable. But even the very preliminary studies embodied in the exercises in this book will surely be of interest to others as well. The other students in the class will certainly want to hear about the experiences of their peers. The people who were studied will probably be very curious to learn what the ethnographer has concluded about them, their beliefs, and behaviors. The scholarly community will want to know about new substantive information, as well as innovations in method, and will be especially concerned with ways in which basic information about social science research has been conveyed to a new generation of students. And perhaps even the general public will want to know what you have found out, particularly if the topic or theme of your research is one of wide interest (such as the suggested oral history project having to do with remembrances of 9/11).

Students often assume that one satisfies all those potential audiences with the same product format. Anyone who hangs around in academe long enough gets into the habit of thinking that a written report (either of article or book length, as the case may be) is the only acceptable way to share one's findings. Worse, we tend to assume that the only acceptable style for such reports is the stilted, jargon-laden genre of "scholarly" prose. It is undeniably true that the academic report is the most widely recognized standard for the dissemination of knowledge, and your instructor will almost certainly expect that the paper(s) you hand in to him or her will follow these conventions. Your instructor will also be aware of professional associations in the various disciplines that have student sections and that would accept outstanding papers to be presented at annual conferences. I hope that some of you take advantage of such opportunities to address your scientific colleagues.

But I also invite you to think outside the box once you have satisfied those traditional academic requirements. For example, your class might put together a panel discussion in which ideas are exchanged among all participants. The quality of such a forum might be enhanced if members of the study community and the general public (e.g., your friends not taking this class) were invited to take part as well.

Or you might want to put together a Web site (or a set of linked Web pages) or an integrated video production that highlights the work you have done this semester.

If the nature of the data you have collected lends itself to visual display, you might want to construct some sort of museum exhibit that would be open to the public.

You can respond artistically to the material, rendering what you have learned in the form of short stories, one-act plays, songs, paintings, dances, puppet shows, mime, and so forth. (For years I have been urging my students to try these expressive forms, and I have received a number of creative and exciting "reports" in the forms of video programs and interactive Web sites. I've had no takers, however, on the puppet show and mime options.)

The point is that different audiences assimilate information in different ways. Academics are primed to expect the scholarly paper and are comfortable reading or listening to such reports even if they find them slightly boring. But others have no similar allegiance to that style of presentation, and if your goal is to share what you have learned, then you need to learn how to be effective as a communicator. After all, ethnography helps us learn about culture, and an important part of culture is how people communicate; learning how to convey information should therefore be an integral part of what you do as an ethnographic researcher. And even if your career plans do not include becoming a professional ethnographer, the skills you have practiced here will no doubt serve you well as you make your own way as an insightful, curious citizen of a globally interrelated world.

So I hope that the course will not end with you simply handing in your papers to your instructor and then moving on. The best ethnography is a kind of ongoing dialogue, and I hope you will be able to take what you have learned and build it into just such an exchange. (And please contact me to let me know if any of you tries a puppet show or mime performance!)

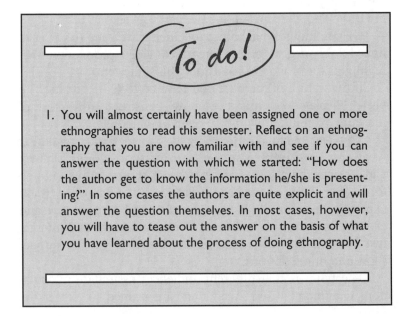

To do!

1. You will almost certainly have been assigned one or more ethnographies to read this semester. Reflect on an ethnography that you are now familiar with and see if you can answer the question with which we started: "How does the author get to know the information he/she is presenting?" In some cases the authors are quite explicit and will answer the question themselves. In most cases, however, you will have to tease out the answer on the basis of what you have learned about the process of doing ethnography.

Additional Reading

The following list is *not* an exhaustive research bibliography. It is simply a selection of items that a beginning student might find useful should he or she pursue the craft of ethnography.

Other Learn-by-Doing Project/Exercise Books

Angrosino, Michael V. 2002. *Doing Cultural Anthropology: Projects for Ethnographic Data Collection*. Prospect Heights, IL: Waveland Press.

Crane, Julia G. and Michael V. Angrosino. 1992. *Field Projects in Anthropology: A Student Handbook*, 3rd ed. Prospect Heights, IL: Waveland Press.

Janesick, Valerie J. 1998. *"Stretching" Exercises for Qualitative Researchers*. Thousand Oaks, CA: Sage.

Mason, Jennifer. 2002. *Qualitative Researching*, 2nd ed. London: Sage.

McCurdy, David W., James P. Spradley, and Dianna J. Shandy. 2005. *The Cultural Experience: Ethnography in a Complex Society*, 2nd ed. Long Grove, IL: Waveland Press.

Wiseman, Jacqueline P. and Marcia S. Aron. 1970. *Field Projects for Sociology Students.* Cambridge, MA: Schenkman.

Personal Reflections on Doing Ethnography

Agar, Michael H. 1980. *The Professional Stranger: An Informal Introduction to Ethnography.* New York: Academic Press.

DeVita, Philip R., ed. 1991. *The Naked Anthropologist: Tales from around the World.* Belmont, CA: Wadsworth.

Van Maanen, John, ed. 1988. *Tales of the Field: On Writing Ethnography.* Chicago: University of Chicago Press.

Ethnographic Methods Textbooks

Agar, Michael H. 1986. *Speaking of Ethnography.* Beverly Hills, CA: Sage.

Berg, Bruce L. 2004. *Qualitative Research Methods for the Social Sciences,* 5th ed. Boston: Pearson.

Bernard, H. Russell. 1988. *Research Methods in Cultural Anthropology.* Newbury Park, CA: Sage.

Creswell, John W. 1998. *Qualitative Inquiry and Research Design: Choosing among Five Traditions.* Thousand Oaks, CA: Sage.

Denzin, Norman K. and Yvonna S. Lincoln, eds. 2003. *Collecting and Interpreting Qualitative Materials,* 2nd ed. Thousand Oaks, CA: Sage.

Fetterman, David M. 1998. *Ethnography Step by Step,* 2nd ed. Thousand Oaks, CA: Sage.

Miles, Matthew B. and A. Michael Huberman. 1994. *Qualitative Data Analysis,* 2nd ed. Thousand Oaks, CA: Sage.

Rossman, Gretchen B. and Sharon F. Rallis. 1998. *Learning in the Field: An Introduction to Qualitative Research.* Thousand Oaks, CA: Sage.

Collections of Writings about Fieldwork Projects

Borzak, Lenore, ed. 1981. *Field Study: A Sourcebook for Experiential Learning*. Beverly Hills, CA: Sage.

Emerson, Robert M., ed. 2001. *Contemporary Field Research*, 2nd ed. Prospect Heights, IL: Waveland Press.

Van Maanen, John, ed. 1983. *Qualitative Methodology*. Beverly Hills, CA: Sage.

For Those Who Want to Exercise Their Creativity in Presenting the Results of Ethnographic Research

Banks, Anna and Stephen P. Banks, eds. 1998. *Fiction and Social Research: By Ice or Fire*. Walnut Creek, CA: AltaMira.

Bochner, Arthur P. and Carolyn Ellis, eds. 2002. *Ethnographically Speaking: Autoethnography, Literature, and Aesthetics*. Walnut Creek, CA: AltaMira.

Ellis, Carolyn and Arthur P. Bochner, eds. 1996. *Composing Ethnography: Alternative Forms of Qualitative Writing*. Walnut Creek, CA: AltaMira.

Sparkes, Andrew C. 2002. *Telling Tales in Sport and Physical Activity: A Qualitative Journey*. Champaign, IL: Human Kinetics.

For the Truly Ambitious

Denzin, Norman K. and Yvonna S. Lincoln, eds. 2000. *Handbook of Qualitative Research*, 2nd ed. Thousand Oaks, CA: Sage.

Schensul, Jean J. and Margaret D. LeCompte. 1999. *Ethnographer's Toolkit* (7 volumes). Walnut Creek, CA: AltaMira.

Index

Access, 5, 20, 25, 27, 59, 62
  to materials and records, 59, 62
  protecting research, 20, 53
  to research populations, 5, 25, 27
Allusion, 47
Analysis, 23, 49, 55–59
Archives, 10, 53, 55, 57–58, 59, 62
Artifact, 18, 56
Audience, 36, 62
Audio recording, 27, 48
Authority, 28

Behavior, 1, 15, 16, 17, 24, 40, 50
Beliefs, 16, 17, 23, 26, 29, 33, 62
Biomedical research, 19, 20
Border identity, 18
Bounded, 24, 25, 26, 40
Bourgois, Philippe, 14
Budget, 25

Communication, 4, 18, 20, 49
Comparative, 14, 38, 40
Complexity, 51
Confidentiality, 20, 21
Contact, 12, 13, 27, 28, 46, 48, 57, 64
Context, 16, 30
Control, 4, 5, 27
Covert, 24
Criteria, 24–26, 31, 35
  conceptual, 26
  definitional, 24, 26
  logistical, 25
Critical thinking, 3, 10
Cultural anthropology, 4, 9, 10
Cultural matrix, 18
Cultural relativism, 17, 18, 21
Culture, 4, 6, 14, 17, 18, 34, 35, 41, 44, 45, 47, 52, 55, 56, 61, 64
  definition of, 4, 17

Dance, 4
Data, 6, 8, 9, 10, 14, 15, 34, 36,
    37, 38, 49, 55, 57, 58, 59,
    60, 62, 63
    and archives, 55–59
    collection techniques, 9, 10,
        15, 36, 49
    comparing, 38
    firsthand, 55, 57
    and generating theory, 15, 34
    recording, 36, 38
    secondary data, 57
    storage, 57
Deinstitutionalization, 12
deRoche, Constance, 16
Descriptive, 2, 6, 51, 57
Design, 5, 6, 39
Diabetes, 13, 16
Dissemination, 62, 63
Dworkin, Gary, 15, 16

Equipment, 27, 48
Ethics, 19
Ethnic group, 17, 26
Ethnography
    collection techniques, 10, 33,
        50
    definition of, 4, 33
    principles of, 11–19
    purpose of, 4, 18, 33
    stereotypes of, 9
Experimental design, 5, 6, 8,
    13, 20
Experimental research, 5
Exploratory interviews, 44, 45,
    49, 50, 51, 52

Facts, 2, 3, 8, 9, 36
Field
    and archived materials, 55, 57
    definition of, 4, 23
    and developing theories, 15

entering the, 26–27
    ethics in, 20
    first contact in, 27–28
    observation in, 34, 38
    research, 5, 6, 7, 8, 25
Films, 4
Findings, presentation of, 4, 10,
    61–64
Focused interview, 11, 12, 15,
    49
Formative theory, 34, 35, 39,
    40, 44, 52, 61

Gender, 6, 17, 30, 58
Grobsmith, Elizabeth, 14
Grounded theory, 15, 21

Hispanic, 17, 26
Historical, 56
Holistic, 16, 21
HRAF, 57
Hypothesis, 6, 50

Identity, 17, 18
In-depth, 44, 51
Inductive, 15, 21
Informed consent, 20, 21, 37
Inquiry, 15, 21, 57
    deductive, 15
    inductive, 15, 21
Insider, 15
Institutions, 11, 16, 35, 56
Instrument, ethnographer as, 6,
    7, 30
Interaction, 35, 44
Internet, 18, 23, 24
Interpretation, 6, 10, 40
Interviews, 10, 12, 15, 16, 18,
    43–51, 52, 53, 59, 62
    conducting, 43–47
    exploratory, 44, 45, 49, 50,
        51, 52

focused, 11, 12, 15, 49
in-depth, 44, 51
open-ended, 6, 15, 44, 51
recording, 48, 49
semi-structured, 49–51, 52, 53
unobtrusive, 38, 39, 40, 61
unstructured, 39, 49
Inventory, 26, 30
IRBs, 19

Jargon, 2, 50, 63
Journal, 22, 30, 37
Judgment, reserving, 3, 19

Key informants, 47, 49
Kinesics, 37, 39, 40
Kinship, 1, 17

Laboratory, 4, 5, 7, 11
Life history, 45, 47, 51, 52
Local, 3, 9, 11, 16, 17, 25, 34,
    47, 52, 56, 58
Location, 24

Maps, 27, 36, 56
Marginalized, 26
Measures, 5, 23, 24
Mental disability, 12, 26, 35
Mental illness, 11
Mental retardation, 11, 26
Method, 4, 8, 9, 10, 13, 62
Murphy, Kathleen, 18
Museum, 4, 19, 56, 63
Music, 4, 23, 25, 52
Mutuality, 13, 21

Nanda, Serena, 56
Narrative, 4, 6, 44, 46, 47, 49, 53
Native American, 14, 25, 56, 58
Nonreactive research, 57, 59
Notes, field, 20, 30, 31, 36, 37,
    38, 39, 40, 48, 57, 61

Observations, 10, 12, 33–45, 55,
    56, 59
structured, 38, 40–41
unobtrusive, 38, 39, 40, 61
unstructured, 39, 49
Oral history, 45, 47, 51, 53, 58,
    62

Participant, 38, 39, 49
Participant observation, 7, 9,
    38–40, 44, 52, 61
Participation, 24, 37–38
Patterns, 6, 16, 17, 25, 34, 35,
    36, 44
Performance, 4, 64
Permission, 53
Poetry, 4
Populations, 11, 14
    marginalized, 26
    selection of, 25–27, 47
    vulnerable, 20
Position, 3, 20, 46
Prisoner, 14
Privacy, 19, 20
Probe, 6, 44, 45, 52
Proxemics, 37, 39, 40
Pseudonym, 37
Public, 4, 13, 16, 19, 24, 26, 37,
    56, 59, 62, 63

Qualitative, 6, 10, 50
Quantitative, 50
Question, 3, 5, 24, 26, 44, 49,
    51, 62, 64

Rapport, 7, 12, 13, 14, 21, 28,
    45
Reflection, 3
Research question, 3, 5, 26, 44,
    51, 62, 64
Researcher
    as instrument, 6, 7, 30

limitations of, 7, 25
personal characteristics of,
    28–30

Sampling, 26
Saturation, 26
Schensul, Stephen, 50
Secondary data, 57, 59
Selection, participant, 25–27,
    47
Setting, 4, 5, 18, 25, 34, 36, 38,
    40, 45, 52, 53, 59, 61
Shandy, Dianna, 18
Small-scale, 3, 25, 34
Space, 24, 36, 37, 38, 40
Status, 13, 20
Stress, 15, 16
Survey, 26, 44, 47, 49
Systems, 4

Team, 10, 25, 38, 50
Theory, 15, 21, 34, 35, 39, 40,
    44, 52, 61
    formative, 34, 35, 39, 40, 44,
        52, 61
    grounded, 15, 21
Tolerance, 7
Tradition, 4, 17
Transcription, 49, 53
Triangulation, 15, 21, 62
Trust, 12, 14

Unit of analysis, 23–26, 29, 61,
    62

Variables, 5, 6, 15, 39, 49
Video, 27, 48, 63
Visual aids, 36, 48, 63